THE RICH FREELANCER

TOP TIPS AND SECRETS TO HELP YOU WORK FROM HOME, AND GET RICH IN THE PROCESS

BRYAN WESTRA

Indirect Knowledge Limited
MURRAY, KENTUCKY

Bryan Westra/Indirect Knowledge Limited
2317 University Station
Murray, KY/42071
www.indirectknowledge.com

Book Layout ©2014 Indirect Knowledge Limited

Ordering Information:
Quantity sales. Special discounts are available on quantity purchases by corporations, associations, and others. For details, contact the "Special Sales Department" at the address above.

The Rich Freelancer/ Bryan Westra. —1st ed.
ISBN-10: 099051322X
ISBN-13: 978-0-9905132-2-3

TABLE OF CONTENTS

Dedication to Jennifer Bonilla

"Either write something worth reading or do something worth writing."

—BENJAMIN FRANKLIN

READ CAREFULLY

Thank you for purchasing my book. It is important for me to thank you, because it means you've entrusted me to teach you something, mostly from my own experience, and believe that it will too do you some good. I really hope it does. If it doesn't I want you to think about this: Many people buy a book, and never fully read it, and much fewer actually put its teachings to any use in their own life. Now, don't mistaken me to say that if you don't use this information now, that it will be a waste of money spent, as I don't believe that information partly studied, and not acted upon yet, is a waste, at all. There is value, whether be intrinsic value, or future value, or indirect value that can be applied to other life events, circumstances, contexts, and so on.

To date I've written and published fifteen books. The fifteen books I've written and published up-until-now have all been longer books that take a lot longer to read through. There is value in these books, that's for sure. I'm proud of what I produce, but not in an egotistical way.

I am extremely passionate about learning and passing on information. I'm an educator in most of what I do professionally. I own a training company in fact, that specializes on teaching people powerful and dynamic communication skills. I went to university for this and after graduating, instead of doing what most of my peers did, I started a business to help other people. I was older when I went to college, so I'd had my days in the workplace (good days and not so good). I wanted to help people rise to the top of their professions. I wanted to help people communicate not only more effectively, but beyond the scope of what some of the best communicators communicate. I believe that 'communication' combined with 'thinking' has the power to take people far in life. My number one principle, even beyond mastering the skills of 'communication' and 'thinking' is 'action'. Let me explain...

I have known many brilliant people in my life who were excellent (above the cut) communicators. They could impress you, get you stirred, and make you believe anything and feel anyway, yet these people I speak of had one major flaw the made them fractionally successful at best—they lacked ACTION.

I was taking my dog 'Foxy-Brown' (Red Australian Cattle Dog) for a walk last week. When I walk, I usually do some of my best thinking. It's a habit I have created for myself. I take my dog for numerous walks each and every day, so as you might imagine I do a lot of thinking. Remember 'thinking' is one part of my success formula. There is a difference between 'thinking' (an action) and 'thought' (a noun). Of course 'action' is another part of my success formula! Thinking is problem solving and developing processes and systems in your head, before you implement them. Thinking allows you to role-play scenarios in your mind, to be able to predict likely outcomes.

But...back to my walk the other day...

I was thinking about 'how' I could get more of my readers to take action and see the results of those actions. Then an idea came to me. I thought, "Hmm...Perhaps I could write some shorter books that were 'how-to' themed, that could be read in an hour or two for busy people or people who don't like to necessarily read." Then I had the idea for this first book strike me. I decided that I would write a book detailing my experiences and insights about working from home as a freelancer.

There's a massive problem most freelancers starting out experience. This problem leads many 'would-be career freelancers' to go back into the workforce only to wind up back miserable again. The problem most new freelancers find out straightaway is that it can be challenging to earn even a minimum wage when they begin working for themselves as a freelancer.

The problem is the model. The model is based around the idea that if a company or individual contracts help it is usually for the purpose of saving money. Companies and individuals like to hire work-at-home freelancers because they typically can get away paying these freelancers much less than what they would have to pay someone hired in-house. They don't for instance have to pay benefits, and because most freelance work is bid on in a freelance marketplace the competition is fierce, and people in India, Indonesia, and other countries where the cost and standards of living are much less will often times bid these jobs for next to nothing. Well, I say 'nothing' but the truth is the little bit they bid is actually quite a significant amount in their home country. The internet has united the world and connected people. Businesses outsource work to countries where people are willing to work for next to nothing. It's win-win for the businesses and those low wage workers, because the businesses save millions on what it would otherwise cost them to hire in-house employees, and the freelancer in a third or fourth world country realizes the benefit of earning a lot more than they would otherwise earn were they to go out and get a job (assuming a job was even available).

Who does get affected are the freelancers in first world countries who must pay a lot more money out to survive. A loaf of bread may cost around .35 cents in India, but in America the loaf I just bought today (standard cheap white bread) was $2.49. Quite a difference in price. I can't live off of earning a couple dollars per hour, and I'd have to work around the clock to probably pay for my daily meals here, so as you see there's a real problem that persists in the world of freelance in America and other first world countries.

Some people will argue with me and say: "Well, it just depends on what you do?" I agree to some extent. If you're a computer programmer who can develop world class software for companies like Microsoft, etc., then yes, you can command a higher freelance wage; however, keep in mind, there are a lot of competition for these jobs too, from programmers and coders in other countries like India. Why pay you $100 per hour, when they can get a guy in India to code just as well for $25 dollars per hour? You get the point.

So anyway, this is what problem I ran into as a freelancer some years back, and I (being the problem solver I am) discovered a way to make it work, and even be more profitable for you than if you were to go back to work in the 'real world'.

This book is short, it didn't cost you much, but don't take that to mean that it possesses any less value than some of the longer books I've written or that you've purchased from other 'how-to' non-fiction authors. It may shock you to learn that it has a significant more value to you, when you stop to consider that it's short, and immediately actionable. This was the whole logic to my 'thinking' last week, regarding how I might be able to teach something incredibly valuable in a very short course that could be implemented immediately.

I'm a fan of P.T. Barnum, and reference him from time to time in my books. I want to finish off this introduction by citing something he wrote in his book, "The Art of Money Getting":

> "LEARN SOMETHING USEFUL Every man should make his son or daughter learn some useful trade or profession, so that in these days of changing fortunes of being rich to-day and poor tomorrow they may have something tangible to fall back upon. This provision might save many persons from misery, who by some unexpected turn of fortune have lost all their means."
>
> —P.T. BARNUM

What you will be learning in this book is something useful. If followed and acted upon it will help you weather the financial climates in the future that may be even less favorable than they are right now. Learning the information in this book will help you to have something to "fall back upon" should something come along to cause you misfortune in some area of your life, someday.

I hope you get immense value from what you're about to learn!

Learn Well! Live Well!

CHAPTER 1

MY STORY

My story begins back in the early 2000s, when I had lost my job as a sales executive for a mid-sized Yellow Pages Directory Company. I'd work for the company for quite some time building up a massive sales territory, only to have that territory taken away from me, and given to one of the owner's sons. I wasn't fired, but rather asked to move on to build up a different territory; probably, so I could build it up, so that someone else could have it later on.

Usually in advertising sales, after about three years or so, once a territory is built up, the sales agent can sit back and enjoy a lavish lifestyle, as he or she's built a strong relationships with his customers, and they continue to buy from him year after year, spending more and more money. That was my case.

Being a sales professional, working out in the field, day in and day out, I was accustomed to working independently and on my own. I was never lonely, because I was constantly focused on earning income, and helping my clients to successfully advertise their businesses in the Yellow Pages directory that I represented.

When I was met with the choice to either move on to another territory or quit, it was a no-brainer for me. I decided that I could do sales on my own, in a different capacity, and earn a substantially larger income, and not have a boss looking over my shoulders, waiting to take my territory away, or rip me off somehow.

Being unemployed for about a month, I became agitated, stressed out, moving toward broke quickly, and feeling as though something had to give, or else I was going to find myself working at some fast food restaurant, or grocery store. I didn't want that. So I turned to the Internet, and discovered there were many business opportunities online.

Most of the people I consulted with about these types of business opportunities cautioned me, telling me that these type of opportunities were generally to get my money, and would only cause me more headaches than what they were worth. I didn't listen. I dabbled in MLM and a couple of network marketing companies, and as my friends and colleagues predicted so correctly, became completely broke! So broke in fact that I literally found myself well-over $250,000 in debt. I owned nothing. I didn't own a car at the time, as I couldn't afford the payments, and so the car was repossessed. I didn't own any real estate or property or the house that I was living in. I was in my late 20s, without an education, and completely broke, and to top it all off the town I lived in was a small town in western Kentucky, in which the only jobs available were fast food restaurants and grocery store stocker positions.

I didn't give up though. I decided that if other people could make money on the Internet that I could too. One day, while surfing around for different opportunities online, I stumbled across a couple of online freelance websites. These freelance websites were designed to partner up freelance experts with companies and individuals who needed specialized services done at a fraction of the rate it would cost them to hire someone in-house. Now I was getting onto something. I instantly signed up for an account on every freelance website that I could find, that didn't cost me money to join. I figured the only thing I had to lose, was the time that I'd invest in setting up the accounts and trying to beg people to contract out and hire me.

After a month of doing freelance work, I quickly discovered some of the truths of freelancing: (a) everybody wants something for next to nothing, (b) if a requester can rip you off, they generally do, and (c) you can work for less than a dollar an hour, and the guy or gal who hired you will still feel cheated, and as though you should have provided them with more value than humanly possible. I saw so many different vantage points of being an online freelance worker, that it nearly drove me insane. It was like living in my rented apartment, full time, rarely leaving, and still feeling as though I was working in a third or fourth world company, with the level of income I was earning. I was working my butt off, and getting nowhere.

The truth of the matter is, I could've worked at one of those fast food restaurants and made a lot more money, than what I was making freelancing. I knew there had to be a better way, but I couldn't see how it was possible for people to be able to stay in their homes work only 8 hours per day, and come out on top at the end of the month; that is, have money left over after bills are paid. I tried everything! I tried network marketing, MLM, freelance websites, affiliate marketing, and the list goes on and on and on, and so on.

So I have this brother, and his name is Brandon, and it just so happen the Brandon happened to be out of work like myself that one juncture. So I was telling him about working online and doing freelance work, and he became very interested as well, and wanted to learn more about it. So he and I decided, perhaps because were so close, that we would attempt to do this online work together, and possibly break the code on how to get rich as a freelancer.

Well we quickly discovered that we got time zones confused, job descriptions confused, and had a few communication problems with clients. If fact, we had this one client who lived in the United Kingdom, and this guy had us calling people on Skype in the United Kingdom trying to sell them real estate which he claimed to own down in Florida; which probably was swampland, or land he didn't actually own, and for some strange, bizarre, reason we actually enjoyed the work, and we found ourselves not minding it at all. The problem was we were getting the time zones mixed up and many of the people we called on, would tell us "yes", and then back out of the deal last minute. Well, we only got paid if we actually close the deal, and to be quite truthful we weren't closing too many deals. At least not enough to pay the bills.

After about a month, of doing this type of work, for this gentleman, we were terminated without notice. We were not paid our last week's earnings, and there was really very little we coud do about it, considering this gentleman was country jumping from Spain to France to the United Kingdom to Germany and every other country you can think of, as any wealthy scam artist might need to do, at least we thought this was the case, and we knew instinctively that we really never stood a chance of finding him. So my brother became hardened at the freelance marketplace, and quickly bowed out, and got a job at one of those fast-food restaurants. He told me I was a foolish for staying in the game. I sort of thought he was right, and afraid that I'd be making a big mistake either way (either working at one of those fast-food restaurants or working online for less than a dollar per hour). However, I knew that many people were earning lucrative incomes working for themselves, out of the comfort of their own home, and others were making such substantial incomes, that they lived in the most immaculate homes I had ever seen. I had to find out what they were doing, because my dream since childhood was to retire early and live out the rest of my days happy wealthy, and hopefully wiser.

I made a lot of painful mistakes as a freelancer. I also made a lot of mistakes (mostly financial) trying my luck at network marketing and MLM companies. I sponsored people here and there, and before I had my residual income check, the new recruit had dropped out. I was left still having to pay my monthly franchise fee, even though I didn't earn any money that month, and not to mention the hundreds of wasted hours spent coaxing people into joining with me—in hopes of getting rich quick.

Was I stupid? A lot of people thought so. I may have been for a good bit of the journey. Okay…most of the journey, but one thing I was still certain of was that I could do what anybody else could do (a mantra repeated over and over and over to me by my father growing up). He always said, "If somebody else can do it, so can I." I believed I could do the same.

When is enough—enough? I don't have the answer for you on that one, but I would say I had plenty of opportunities to give up, but never did. I am on the extreme end of seeing things through to the end. I've wound up losing a lot by this mentality, but I have gained a lot as well. I think most people give up too early; perhaps, I give up too late.

CHAPTER 2

THE BENEFITS OF FREELANCE WORK THAT BECOME RESOURCES FOR WEALTH

Many of the network marketing companies I joined had a dimension to them that focused on personal development. One company I partnered with was in truth a personal development company. I think one reason for these companies emphasizing personal development is because they know if they can get people to change their mindset to an "I can" type of mentality, they stand a greater chance of keeping the new recruit in the game longer; meaning, more profit for them.

In marketing they have a term called 'customer lifetime value', which simply stated is the value of a customer over the time they remain a customer. It is this way in network marketing also. A recruit that stays a recruit longer is more profitable for the network marketing company. The same goes for members who recruit people into their down lines. If I recruit someone and they remain a partner longer, it means more money in my pocket.

Unfortunately, many people take to personal development to their detriment, and I'm a victim also, I must admit. However, I believe this only applies to the loss of staying in a network marketing company in which you'll likely never make much money, and not the part concerning the benefits of personal development.

Personal development gives you strategy for how you plan out your life. This can be as simple as how you plan your day, or as complicated as how you plan your life. There are many excellent things you gain as a benefit of immersing yourself in personal development—for example, you gain the advantage of continually learning, planning, and strategizing your life until it become more and more in alignment with what you want.

I studied Tony Robbins, Michael Losier, Brian Tracy, and many other gurus of personal development while on my journey to becoming rich as a freelancer. I can't express how important personal development was for me, as it kept me constantly learning, and improving on the ways that I earned money working from home.

When you are a freelancer, working through many of these freelance websites (e.g., oDesk.com, Fiverr.com, Guru.com, Freelancer.com, Elance.com, iWriter.com, and others) you learn how to do many things that you otherwise would never take the time to learn. Learning such skills makes you more valuable and more likely to get freelance contracting jobs.

Some of the skills I learned were: graphic design, search engine optimization, computer programming, writing, sales and marketing, and many others. I have done freelance work for other people and companies doing exactly these types of jobs. I learned as I went. I discovered I fancied the constantly changing types of work that I did. I got bored writing 500 word SEO articles, and so I'd switch to designing book covers, or designing graphics for websites. I did all sorts of different types of jobs.

There was a constant problem that persisted however: I was still always, it seemed, working for peanuts, and never getting myself ahead, let alone rich. This frustrated me to no end, especially when Brandon would show me a $500 dollar paycheck he'd earned that week, and I knew I'd only earned a hundred or so. He could pay his bills, but I could not. I was feeling the pressure to do better and better, but the truth was I was working around the clock making nothing, while my brother only worked 40 hours per week and had five times the money I had.

It looks glamorous from the outside looking in, but the reality is, you work more as a freelancer and make quite a lot less if you're not careful or don't know how the real money is made.

I've always been an experimenter. I test everything. It's in my nature. I once figured out that I could be a virtual assistant for five companies at the same time, charging each of them $3 per hour, and actually earn $15 dollars per hour. This made more sense to me than working for one client for $5 per hour (which was usually the case).

One client I had was a guy from Australia who owned an e-commerce website, who hired me for $300 dollars to write a sales script for his future freelance telesales force. I spent a full week working and revising his script, each time as he requested, and then in the end he never paid me. I wasn't about to travel to Australia just to kick his butt! So you see, there're many challenges one becomes confronted with when working as a freelancer.

Let's not harp on the negative, as I think I've clarified this much for you already, and chances are if you're reading this book, you've probably already experimented and tested the waters as a freelancer and so probably know all-to-well what I'm talking about. Let's instead look at some of the advantages.

I've already expressed how you'll learn a lot of new skills inadvertently as a freelancer. I sure did anyway. One thing I did, and recommend you adopt as well, is to watch YouTube videos on whatever it is you need to learn. I really do believe you can learn just about anything you want to simply by watching YouTube videos. There's a video on just about anything you want to learn how to do. I also have read somewhere recently that people learn more through watching videos than they do in a college classroom.

Another benefit to freelancing is that you'll learn many new types of technologies. I learned many of Adobe's suite of programs, as well as Microsoft Office's suite of programs. I know Excel, Word, PowerPoint, Publisher, like the back of my own hand. I never would have had a use for them before becoming a freelancer. Knowledge is power, because you can take your learnings and think of them as 'resources' which can be applied to making money—real money!

Try not to think about the ridiculous small amounts of money I've mentioned I made, because I promise you making this little bit of money has a great advantage that is all part of this system I'm going to teach you in the forthcoming chapters. You'll see why earning so little is so advantageous soon, I promise. For now, only think about the benefits and how those benefits can be utilized as resources in the near future to help you become richer than you'd ever thought possible.

CHAPTER 3

NLP AND ME

I know this title is a bit weird. I mentioned earlier how I was a student of personal development that was encouraged by the network marketing companies I had chosen to partner with. One of the guys in personal development that was instrumental in my change of mind from being in a poverty mindset to being in a rich person's mindset was Tony Robbins. He's also called Anthony Robbins as well.

Tony wrote a book on Neuro-Linguistic Programming several years ago I read his book and couldn't put it down until I finished. He talked about ideas I'd never heard of before. One of these ideas was how there is no failure, or feedback. This is a common NLP presupposition. A presupposition by the way is a belief one assumes to be true (even if it isn't).

One of the other presuppositions is that you always have all the resources at your disposal to obtain whatever it is you desire and want. In most cases this relates to goal-planning. When you're planning your next move, one of the first things you do is take an assessment of all your resources in order to plan appropriately and get what you want out of life. This usually is intended to get you one step closer toward the direction of your next goal.

When you're talking about making more money than you're currently making working from home as a freelancer, one thing you can do, which I did, was to take stock of all my resources. When I did this I realized I had a lot more resources than I'd realized. For starters I owned a laptop with a webcam and microphone and speakers. I also owned a lot of really cool software (I used this for my freelance gigs mostly). I also had no schedule except the one I set for myself. I also had no place I necessarily had to be. I also knew I was strong as a writer. I also knew I was making around $100 dollars per week (enough for groceries).

Here's what I did after taking stock of all my resources: I decided I wanted to go back to college. Granted I was in my late 20s and most of the people I'd graduated high-school with had already either gotten a college degree and were working in a higher paying job, or else had forgone college and were working making a significantly higher wage than just the minimum wage. I was making less than minimum wage.

I almost felt like I shouldn't go to college, because I felt like it was more or less too late to be doing the whole college thing. I still wanted to achieve my goal of getting a college degree. I wasn't the brightest crayon in the box either, and so this made me feel apprehensive about attending.

I got enrolled and started classes, and graduated three years later Magna Cum Laude. I lived on financial aid checks and used this money resourcefully to start my own company. The company is one I still own today: www.indirectknowledge.com. The company specializes in teaching people NLP and Hypnosis and Sales, Marketing, and Interpersonal Communication skills.

After I finished my bachelors I became the first person in my immediate family to earn a college degree. I was on cloud nine, because I knew I had accomplished a goal of mine. I used my personal development resources, past experiences in sales and marketing, to earn a B.A. in Organizational Behavior with a minor in Sales Leadership. I guess I did have all the resources I needed.

Then I didn't stop there, I went on to earn an MBA in Marketing. I graduated from a distinguished private school with a 4.00 GPA (Summa Cum Laude). I was going places with my education. The problem, however, is that university institutions are designed to prepare you to go out and get a job, and earn a wage. I didn't, and never intentioned on going to work for somebody else, ever again. I wanted to work from home and be successful and earn more than most everyone else I knew. This might not be saying too much considering most of the people I knew were extremely broke, borrowing tiny bits that they could off of other broke people.

So I had accomplished some personal goals that were more for me and not so much about what I planned to do with the education after receiving it. After graduation I learned that I didn't have any more 'supportive' income coming in anymore, and that student loans had to be repaid six months later. I was panicked, because I had an extreme amount of student loan debt to repay. I started questioning quickly if the education was worth it or not.

Once again I found myself with too much time on my hands and very little money. I knew I needed to do something quick—but what?

I decided, once again, to take an assessment of my resources, to determine what the best approach to take would be for becoming wealthy while being able to work from home. I decided something profound, and by making a simple decision to tweak my thinking, I could generate an abundance of wealth—all online—easier than most people think possible. I'm going to share this strategy with you in this book...Be patient with me.

CHAPTER 4

RESIDUAL ASSETS

T aking stock of every resource I had I quickly learned that I had, once again, a lot more resources than I thought I had. For one, I had knowledge about network marketing and the principle that underlies it. Namely, leveraging a little bit of money and using it and other resources to produce residual income.

Why Do You Need To Know About Residual Income?

Residual income simply stated is money you make on a recurring basis, usually month to month, from work you did a long time ago. For example, in network marketing you might pay $100 dollars to get started in a business, in which the company furnishes all the marketing materials you need (including a product to sell) to recruit other people beneath you to sell the exact same product. You earn money when you sell a product, but because you've now recruited a sales force beneath you, you in a sense profit like a sales manager would for a company. Every time one of your personally sponsored recruits makes a sale, you also make a sale. I have made more money in network marketing recruiting others and from their sales, than I have ever made off of my personal sales. This doesn't make me a bad sales person, it simply makes me a better sales manager and sales trainer, so to speak.

The residual income that comes from this type of network marketing setup is one that allows you to generate income when other people make sales, even if you do not. So in this regard you make a profit, even when you don't do the work. Not bad, eh?

In writing, authors earn what's known as royalties. These are essentially percentages of book sales that they earn on a regular recurring basis, long after their books are written. In other words, they wrote the book one time, yet profit off of it; let's say, forever! It is the same as the profits a network marketer earns residually from the earlier efforts of building a long down line of successful network marketers.

A residual asset is one that you set-it and forget-it. You do the work once, but continue to profit off the result over and over and over again. This can be duplicated also, meaning you can continue to create more and more residual assets that compound one-on-top of one another. In a relatively short period of time it is possible to have enough of these residual assets set-up that you can rake in some quite amazing income.

What Do You Need To Know About Setting-Up Residual Assets?

To set up a residual asset you need to know a couple of things. First you need to know how lucrative or potentially lucrative the asset is. Second you need to know how long and is it worth your time to set up the asset. Third you need to know or at the very least have an idea of how long the asset will be around generating you passive residual income.

I mentioned earlier about a network marketing company I partnered with that was a personal development company. This particular company didn't have a great residual income component, but even worst the company was out of business three years after I joined, and when they went away, so did my passive residual income (regardless how small it was). What can I say, these types of things happen, and they're not all that too uncommon in fact.

The most important part of my strategy concerning setting up residual assets is to diversify. Any half-way decent stock advisor will advise his or her client to diversify their investment portfolio to shelter them from huge losses. You can have one stock in your portfolio take a dump, but with a well-diversified portfolio you can weather the storm, and make up for the huge loss else-where in your portfolio usually. The same is true of my strategy. You must set up many, many, income streams, and not all from the same river.

If you do this, you'll start to receive a tiny check here, and a tiny check there, and over time these tiny checks collectively add up to a lot of money (depending of course on what you think a lot is). None the less, for most of you reading this book, I'm sure my idea of a lot isn't too far off the radar compared to yours. It is still subjective however, so just consider a lot to be whatever you want it to be.

How To Create A Residual Income Empire

There are many ways to create residual income: My way won't be necessarily your favorite method. I will share my way, however. I'll also give you some ideas to get your brain working, but it will ultimately be up to you to decide how you want to approach setting up your own residual empire.

When I first got started earning residual income I earned them from the network marketing company I first joined. The money kept coming in from the work that I did early on. This is a concept you really need to get your mind wrapped around. The way to fail quickest at my sys-tem of wealth creation is to procrastinate. When you're working for yourself, and you don't have a 'boss' to report to, it is too easy to do what so many people do, which is to do very little, or have this mindset that you can post pone what you need to do until later. Procrastination is something P.T. Barnum talks about in his book: The Art of Money Getting. He says, "Young men after they get through their business training, or apprenticeship, instead of pursuing their avocation and rising in their business, will often lie about doing nothing." I'm telling you essentially the same thing today.

Here's the deal, you have to, right now, realize that to make my system work for you, you have to, in fact MUST, take upfront action. To the extent that you can take massive action immediately, will be the extent that you can most benefit from my system. It will also mean the faster your realized result. In other words, this isn't me telling you what most employers and people who work for a living would tell you: They would tell you, "Well, to get ahead, you have to go to college for an extended period of time, then take a job at the bottom of the corporate structure, and then work really, really, really hard for a period of several more years, and then, and only then, perhaps, if you're one of the lucky ones, be able to rise to the top, and start earning a decent wage." I'm telling you actually the reverse, which isn't necessarily easier, but its: You must take massive action now, and super-duper quickly, so that you can get out of poverty or mediocrity as soon as humanely possible. This isn't the detour route, most people tell you to take, this is the shortest route in the fastest time...we're flying, not driving to our destination. And when you wake-up from your refresher nap, we'll be there.

Now let's board the plane...

The first step you must take is to determine where you want to invest your time (and possibly a little money) to realize a residual income. Now I mentioned my preferences may not be desirable to you, as something else might be. I am a passionate writer and would love to do little else besides write books all day long and earn a fantastic income from the royalties from those books. Writing isn't for everybody though. A lot of people would hate sitting behind a laptop writing all day long for hours on end. I love it. The royalties I make from books I've previously written, as well as courses, flashcard decks, and other training aids, is quite nice, I must admit. But, But, But...It wouldn't be for everybody.

You can however hire people to ghost write for you, and then hire somebody else to do the editing, and hire somebody else to design book covers, and hire...you get the idea...and then self-publish these books on Amazon and other bookseller sites and enjoy the long term residuals you'll earn from work somebody else has done. This is actually a 'part' of my freelance formula, and I'll talk about how you can do this, or aspect of it, and create a residual empire quickly, here in a moment.

Right now, though, understand that there are many places online and off-line that provide an opportunity for you to earn residual income. You can join a network marketing company, and build a strong down line, and each month enjoy a nice hefty residual check or direct deposit payment that like magic shows up month after month after month (even when you've stopped building your down line and now are soaking up rays of sunshine on a beach somewhere). Residual income is a must for the freelancer.

The second step is to realize that you have a many an outlet to create residual income for yourself. As a freelancer you're online a lot, doing your thing, and this means you can do regular activities that create residual income for yourself. You can for instance create a FREE YouTube channel and start promoting affiliate offers, through self-branding yourself as an expert in whatever offers you're presenting to people. Usually, educational information is a huge seller, and a good direction to go. This is because we live in the 'Information Age' now, and it's all about learning and acquiring skills to be more innovative and to improve a process. If you can help somebody learn a skill you've learnt, then it becomes possible for you to profit as a result. The more people you help, the more income you generate.

The key here is to take massive action and setup as many streams of income as you can. And, I certainly mean RESIDUAL income streams. Because, you can sell a product once, and make money; however, I think you'll agree that creating one product, and offering it up for sale, to a worldwide marketplace of potential customers, will yield you far greater results over time.

Let me give you an example, a personal example at that, to share with you how I went about taking massive action to create multiple streams of income.

For starters, let me just say that I stumbled upon this very system I'm teaching you here in this book. What I did was start placing affiliate links to offers on Click-Bank.com, JVZoo.com, CommissionJunction.com, and other affiliate offers from products I had bought and considered a good value for the money. As a freelancer, I bought books (like the this one...well, not *exactly* like this one), and video courses, and all sorts of different training products that I thought would help alleviate the learning curve for me so that I could begin making money faster as a freelancer.

When I found a program or product that worked well and I considered valuable, I would create a YouTube.com video about it, and simply place my affiliate link in the comments section below the video. Whenever somebody stumbled across my video and liked my honest appraisal of the product, and they wanted it too, they would purchase through my affiliate link.

I did this, truthfully, just to help people out. I'm an educator and I know there's a lot of junk out there, and so I like to help people sort through the clutter and noise.

At the time I didn't realize what would eventually happen. It was a year or so later and I was earning regular commissions from these affiliate sales. The commissions kept increasing as I continued putting out more YouTube.com videos.

It's easy to make a YouTube.com video: It simply takes a webcam on a laptop, and you speaking into your computer's microphone. Then uploading the video, or you can even record directly through YouTube's site. My next book I plan to write will be all about capitalizing through YouTube.com and the many secrets I have discovered through experimenting and testing YouTube.com as a marketing channel. I hope if you like this book, you'll take the time to purchase that one also. You'll love the approach and how easy it is to profit from YouTube.com. For now, what I'm telling you is exactly what I did. Just know that there are better ways than this way, but I have to tell it like it was, not what I would do different now.

Now, as a freelancer most of the work I did day-in-and-day-out was article writing for companies, graphic design work, telesales, and being a virtual assistant to small business owners. This type of work didn't really pay the bills so well, but got me by for a period of time until I started mysteriously getting all these residual payments from those affiliate links I placed on YouTube.com.

What happened a year later was that I was earning more income (I promise you this) from the residual income payments than I was actually earning as a freelancer. I would have never stumbled upon doing this though had it not been for doing those freelance jobs, because working a fulltime job I simply would not have made the time to post YouTube videos, let along affiliate offers, because the affiliate offers I was posting were ones that I believed in and knew had tremendous value. These were actually products that helped me become a more profitable freelancer.

So you see, this was all a big accident...

Now something else happened too, which melts into this system I'm exposing you to. I did a lot of freelance jobs for network marketers. These guys and gals were hiring me for a little bit of money to write articles for their blogs, produce green-screen videos, and create a wide array of different graphics for their websites, books, and so on. These were actually some of my best customers, because they knew something I didn't know. Which was it was actually more profitable for them to hire me and other freelancers to work for them than it was for them to do all this work on their own. And, keep in mind, many of these marketers were no dummies and knew how to do, and had done previously, the type of work they were hiring out to freelancers.

At the time I thought, "Gee…these guys/gals are paying me to do this for them. Great for me!" What I didn't come to grips with was the fact that they knew something I didn't know, which was that if they hired me and many other people for very little money to do various freelance jobs, that they could produce an entire product of high quality within a matter of a single day. I'm talking they could hire me to write a 2000 word article for $15, and hire nine more freelance writers to do exactly the same, and they'd have essentially a 20,000 word book, that could be sold on Amazon.com, SmashWords.com, and other sites, not to mention their own blogs and affiliate sites like ClickBank.com, etc. etc. etc.

They could also hire someone to design a book cover, which could be turned into website graphics for a sales page. And, they could outsource the job of creating a click-bank.com 'sales' and 'thank-you' page needed to sell in the online affiliate marketplace. Then to top it off these guys/gals could rely on affiliates with huge email lists to send out emails to people all over the world about the e-book, and rake in tens of thousands of dollars in a few short days.

So who was really making the money here? Was it me making a hit-or-miss $15 per day writing a 2000 word article, which at the time would take me four or five or six hours to write depending on the subject matter, or them, who were making residual income for years to come from paying altogether less than a couple hundred dollars that we recouped in a week or so, easy?

I didn't know all these secrets back then. I thought at the time I had the upper hand and was the one making the money, but I had no idea that the person hiring me was actually the one making all the money, and not me really.

So what does all this add up to? It adds up to the fact that you can make a killing as a freelancer; however, you need to exploit what's already right in front of you, which is the huge marketplace of competing freelancers who are willing and wanting to outbid everybody else in the marketplace in order to make a buck and hour doing something that any normal person would insist on making $20 or more bucks an hour doing. In other words, you need to see your competition as a resource and not a liability. When I realized this, I started making a lot of money working from home as a freelancer. My freelancing however became freelancing for my own self.

You're probably wondering right now if I even wrote this book, am I right? Well, if I am not, I am now at least, right? That's one for you and one for me, so we'll just say we're even. To answer that question though: I am not having this book ghost written. I write my own books, because I LOVE WRITING! Remember, I started off freelancing because I wanted to get into the world of writing articles for major publications—and I still write for major periodicals and newspapers today. Why would I want to stop what I love doing? I don't do it for the money. After all, a $1 per article is what I used to earn, and only churn out a couple per day. I was called 'crazy' by family members and friends. I nearly went broke, and would have, had it not been for the affiliate offers I presented on YouTube.com.

The last think I want to cover in this section of this chapter is network marketing. I told you earlier that I worked for a lot of these internet marketers. In fact some of them were major players online. Individuals who had made millions of dollars exploiting the power of the internet. Because of my associations with these individuals, and casual (non-salesy) conversations I would have, I decided on my own accord, without being manipulated or having my arm twisted, that network marketing was the way to go. If you don't think it is, then that's your prerogative. There's a reason, however, that Donald Trump, started a network marketing company—there's money to be made!

By being a freelancer I had the time to recruit people into my network marketing company. I made a lot of friends. I had a few people curse me on the phone, but overall it was a positive experience, fun, and educational. I also, after a period of nine months or so, started really getting good at prospecting and selling my opportunity over the phone. I even created a powerful system to train my down line that turned into a considerable amount of more residual income for me. I wrote a book explaining exactly how I did this, which, if you're interested, you can purchase directly from Amazon.com here: http://amzn.com/0989946479. The system works, and after you get this book, using it in conjunction with this book here, you'll really see your income increase and sky-rocket. But, not everybody is ready to take on the world of network marketing. And, that's fine, we all make our own decisions.

What Other Ways Might You Harness The Power Of This Information?

The truth is you have lots of options. Not everybody is going to come from my exact background. I've known freelancers who don't even have internet and find themselves sneaking off to the local public library or some coffeehouse to borrow their Wi-Fi connection to make money freelancing. Whatever your circumstance will determine how you approach this information.

I don't like to simply give you the answers, but rather position what I've done more generally, because when I do this, you, and other readers, start 'thinking' and when you do, you start coming up with brilliant ideas that even I haven't thought of before. This makes you an innovator, and us colleagues. All I have, above you, might (maybe not though) be only a bit more experience and know-how. I'm just an ordinary, average of the most average, guys you'd ever meet. I happen though to love working from home. I love, love, love, love, love, love, LOVE, it!!!!

I want to see you make money with my system, should you decide to adopt it as your own, or modify it to fit your particular needs.

I think one of the main things you'll want to take into consideration with this system and the information I've presented and laid out for you in this chapter, is that simple is better. You can write a novel in a year, but it doesn't guarantee it will be a bestseller or that you'll even make any money off of it. Or, you can be like those guys/gals who hired me to write articles for them, and have a product not only created, but for sales in an open marketplace within a single day, marketed by some of the best internet marketers on the planet, and be making a killing by tomorrow. I've seen this happen.

So simple is better. You want to also utilize the problem of competition in the freelance marketplace to your advantage. You want to hire people for a few dollars to do something that will net you thousands of dollars in return over the next several months. This is where the money is. Also, when some of these other freelancers have given up and gone back to work, other newbies will be entering this same freelancers dream-world environment and unbeknownst to them you'll be able to hire them for a fraction of the cost it would take to do it yourself, have it done

faster and probably better, and be making money tomorrow.

The old adage: Keep It Simple Silly (or Stupid?), is so,
so, so, true today. A simple system will make things easier
for you, and help you to profit fast, and without all the
headaches. The key thing to remember is that massive action means rolling out a huge amount of residual assets in
the shortest time frame possible. The more assets you
own, the more money you're bound to make. It just makes
sense. One way of looking at these residual assets is to
think about owning rental properties. If you own one
rental you'll be able to make some money. If you own 100
rentals you'll have so much money coming in you can
quickly and efficiently expand to 1000 rentals quickly. In
other words, when you have one YouTube.com video
with one affiliate link present, you'll eventually, though I
can't promise how soon, make some money. If you have
100 YouTube.com videos with affiliate links to products
you're recommending your viewers to click on and purchase, then you'll unquestionably make a lot more affiliate
sales. It takes time to produce products and YouTube videos, but, even so, some people will jump on the bandwagon and go to work, while others will take their slow-
sweet-time. I'm suggesting you jump on the bandwagon.
Also, important to note, is that you will likely make a
larger substantial income writing shorter books with
20,000 words, than you will writing a book on the same
topic that is 100,000 words. The reason for this is, it will
take you longer to write 100,000 words, and less time to

write 20,000 words. In fact, you will be able to write five 20,000 word books in the same time it takes you to write one 100,000 word book, and the five books of a shorter page count will yield you more opportunities to profit from the ongoing residual royalties from these books. This reflects the real estate rental property metaphor I presented, where five books equals five rental properties, where as one 100,000 word book still only equals one rental property. You'll make more on five rentals usually than you will on only one rental.

So this gets your mind working, doesn't it? You know that you can do more sometimes with less, and the whole objective here is to make a lot of money fast. The perfectionist doesn't win with this system; it's the person who takes decisive smart action.

Final Purport

We covered a lot of ground in this chapter. Primarily you learned how to implement a simple system for generating massive profits fast. This system of mine requires you to do a bit of thinking and a lot of massive action. It means you need to decide what it is you want to promote or sell that has a residual component attached, and go after it. I also taught you the value of diversification. You want to have multiple channels where the money is coming in from. You can market on YouTube as I did, these affiliate offers, or you can write short sweet e-books that sell over and over and over again. The choice is up to you what you want to promote. You can take a day to think about all this and come up with some ideas that work for you. Then you can take the freelance marketplace you've been working out of and exploit the competition, by making them create your residual income producing products, which will get you rich—not them.

CHAPTER 5

BLOGGING

When I started freelancing I didn't know the first thing in the world about blogging. I thought it was something people setup to do personal journaling so that they could tell the world all about themselves. I wasn't at all interested in doing that.

Blogging though isn't that at all. It's actually an online presence you set up to talk about whatever you're passionate about. For me this was sales and marketing. I first tried a free Wordpress.com blog, and later learned that setting up a self-hosted Wordpress.org Blog was better, because you had more liberties to sell and market things on your personally hosted blog. This is what I opted to set-up.

Now I won't get into the instructional aspects of how to setup a self-hosted blog in this book. You can very simply visit YouTube.com and learn from the many tutorials on there, but what I do want to talk about is what happened as a result of starting to blog.

Blogging gave me an outlet to share value with other people. The value was free, of course, because, I mean, after all, who would want to pay for what you know? I was a little naïve you might say.

But, I started blogging, and daily I found that this was somewhat therapeutic for me. I'm someone who likes to talk a lot, and most people are turned off by a chatty-Cathy. I think one reason I liked to talk a lot is because in sales I had this incredible habit of listening to my prospects—listening is actually the key to making sales. Sales people who talk too much, and listen little, don't typically make it long in sales.

When I wasn't on a sales call, back at my house, I would tell my better-half all about my day, about my techniques which closed sales, and all the stuff she didn't want to hear, but listened while tuning me out. She used to tell me: "You talk more than any guy I know!" And, perhaps she was right. I had to have an outlet, and blogging became that outlet for me. So it was very therapeutic, and helped eliminate my talking too much to others.

I started blogging every day. This was a habit I formed early on. I didn't think much of it being a habit, but one day, Jennifer and I were down at the lake, swimming in the Tennessee River, and I realized I didn't blog that day. There was a discomfort that rose up inside me. As soon as I got home, I cranked out another blog post.

Over time, the posts added up. The blog, by the way, was me teaching secret sales techniques to anyone interested in sales and marketing. I loved being in sales, but loved helping others even more. That part of my life was behind me; the going from sales call to sales call, selling Yellow Pages advertising. I knew I could help a lot of other people who were struggling in sales, so I decided to tell all, and see if anyone was interested.

People were interested, I found. I eventually received an email from someone asking me to compile all my blog posts into a book. I was sort of shocked. They told me that if I would do it, regardless how generic it turned out to be, that they'd buy it. I thought, what a brilliant idea: And that's exactly what I did. The book sold lots of copies, and I knew I was on to something.

I have learned a lot of secrets to blogging for profit and I plan to write a book on the subject at some point in the future. There are several good books already out on the subject matter; however, I have some secrets I've not learnt anywhere, except through experimenting and testing. Be on the lookout for that book, when it arrives.

Where I'm going with all this is, you can create a blog, and integrate your marketing through your blog. This is something you should underscore. Marketers are always trying to centralize their marketing efforts, and few think to do this through a blog platform. It can be done, and done well.

Integrating marketing simply means that all your marketing messages and channels can be linked together and help each other out. By having a Wordpress.org self-hosted blog you can develop it so that when you create a new blog post that it gets sent out to Facebook.com, Twitter.com, and other social media sites. You can also add plug-ins that will let you allow others to post comments on your blog. This is a great way to stay in touch with your niche market, and it builds incredible 'goodwill' with your marketplace.

You can also integrate your product offerings (another aspect of marketing) on your blog, which can link back to affiliate offers, your YouTube channel, Amazon products, and you can most certainly, and I advise, sell your products directly through your blog.

There are many ways to monetize a blog. One way is allow Google to place AdSense ads on your blog, and whenever someone clicks the advert you get a tiny commission. I also utilize banner ads which link to affiliate offers. Whenever somebody clicks on an ad, and they buy what the affiliate offer is selling, I get a piece of the pie. You only have to do a little bit of due-diligence to come up with creatively tasteful ways to monetize your blog, and then drive traffic to your blog.

Driving traffic to your blog can come through paid and organic traffic sources. You can write blog articles for other blogs that link back to yours. When visitors to those other blogs read your article, and click a link, and come to your blog, perhaps they'll become a new subscriber, possibly even a new customer.

What I did to drive traffic was simply to write blog articles. I did no paid advertising whatsoever, and today I average 50+ visitors per day—ever day! This creates a lot of sales for me, and helps support my lifestyle. Don't forget however that my system is founded on diversification. You start doing freelance jobs, to learn new skills. Then you transition to hiring your competition in the overpopulated freelance marketplaces to do 'cheap' freelance work for you, so that you can create quick massive residual assets that keep compounding wealth for you, far better than any run-of-the-mill investments out there (e.g., stock market, real estate, etc.). Incidentally, it is worth mentioning that you are investing in assets that are most often 'free' to setup and take advantage of; namely, because they only require your time or you hiring a cheap freelancer to do the work for you—in which case you're simply managing the efforts of other people, ensuring they do a good job for you.

Have a think about this, because let's say you go to work every day at some job, and have more money to invest in stocks and bonds at the end of the month, so you can save for retirement (possibly!). You still have to do a lot of work to get into those investments, like hiring a financial advisor that isn't in his position for commissioned stock trades (he/she is by the way!), and then you have to do your own due diligence. I don't know about you but those prospectuses are a lot of really fine small print—I'm not reading all that jazz, and I bet you aren't either. If you do happen to be one of the few that take out the magnifying glass, you're still sitting for long hours upon hours just to ensure you're not getting ripped off. Is it worth it? I'll let you answer that!

Residual assets are awesome. You 'set-it' and 'forget-it' and that's all you do, except for collect your direct deposits, and pay your taxes. Most importantly you're likely earning a lot more interest off of each dollar you invest, and even more so probably earning money on no money you invest. That's a pretty sweet gig if you think about it.

Blogging is your corporate offices. It's the place online where everything else gets run through. You have plugins for analytics and predictive analytics even. This helps you measure where you're residual portfolio is best performing or underperforming and gets you thinking about how to make that monthly net total rise higher and higher.

First it's getting that first $100 dollars in residual income coming in month after month. Then its $500, then $1000, then $5000, then $10,000, and then whatever you want to aim for. You can be earning in a month what many people can only hope to earn in a year—even two or three years (or 10 years for that matter). All because you acquired the healthy habit of blogging regularly.

What if you hate the idea of writing blog articles? I think you know the answer to this: You simply hire someone for a little bit of money on one of the online freelance marketplaces to write the articles for you. It really is that simple!

If you want to take a quick peak at my blog, you'll see how I have mine setup. The blog has products for sale on it (hint hint!...just kidding!).

CHAPTER 6

WHY I STILL DO FREELANCE

I still do freelance work. A lot of the freelance work I do is article writing, transcription work, and graphic design. I don't make a lot off the jobs I do, but this isn't why I do them. You see I enjoy the work, but there's a greater reason behind why I still do this type of work, as opposed to simply living off the residual assets I've already setup for myself.

The reason might surprise you: I do freelance to keep myself learning. I figure it's a 'paid' education. The work involves constantly learning new technologies, solving complex business problems for other business owners and entrepreneurs, and staying abreast of the latest trends. This last one—staying abreast of the latest trends—is the most valuable and profitable reason I continue doing freelance work for other people.

I'm a writer. I write books, e-books, articles, sales copy, and more. Many of my best ideas and insights come from working other peoples' projects. I learn what's trending and popular and being written about when I work for my competition.

That's right! I learn what my competition is doing by working for them. When they want me to write articles or e-books for them about a particular topic, I have to do the research on that topic, and so I get paid to learn about something I'm going to eventually write about myself, and position better than theirs. When I do this, I can create a better product, because I know what their product consists of; namely because I created it.

All the research is done, all I have to do is take my compiled notes and write a better book and position it better in front of the market. When I do this I undercut them and make more money.

You want to know the best part? It's a secret! You want me to share it?

Okay. Okay! The secret is this: When I'm working for my competition they usually know a great or at least a fair bit about the topic they want me to write on. Because of this I am able to pick their brain. They think they're consulting and educating (helping me essentially) to create the best product possible for them. What they're actually doing, however, is teaching me about the subject matter, and they're spinning ideas out to me. I take these ideas (the good ones) and use them in my own product, which I create after creating theirs.

So the power of continuing to do freelance is that you stay on top of your competition and top them. When you do this, it gives you the edge, and the opportunity to capitalize and make better money.

Now, don't take this the wrong way: I don't cheat my customer, even though they're my competition. I simply take their money, and give them what they pay for. Then I go behind them and create a better product on my own. It's business. In business you have to create a better mousetrap than your competition and people will buy it. And, they do! I can tell you this from experience.

I know what you're thinking: What happens when I outsource my work projects to other freelancers? Don't they do the exact same thing?

The answer is no, not usually! Why? Well, it has to do with the strategy I'm rolling out to you. Nobody, except you (and other readers reading this book) know about this strategy. Be glad you've bought this book. It is filled with lots of gold nuggets that will get you rich, if you follow the advice.

Another reason nobody typically does this to me is because I outsource pieces of my projects to freelancers, and not the whole enchilada. Freelancers who work for me only get a small fraction of the project I'm working on. I do this intentionally.

How?...

Another secret! You want another gold nugget? Okay. Okay! Sure...

So here's how I do this: Let's say I want to write an e-book and sell it on Amazon. I love writing and doing the research, but I know that I can get a lot more books written when I outsource some of the writing. For instance I may write 90% of the book (I'm fast!!), but if my goal to take massive action tells me to write a book a day, then I know to complete this task I may have to hire four or five freelancers to write a 500+ word article, each on a chapter I plan to include in the e-book. So what I do, I and I highly recommend you do as well, is create a template. This template is a format that I am writing and structuring each chapter. Then what I do is take the template and upload it online so my freelancers can download it, and follow the cookie-cutter template. It's hard to mess up a template (not impossible though). Here's what I do though: I get the freelancers to write the boring or highly technical chapters I don't feel like writing, which will take me a lot more time, simply because I don't enjoy writing on 'x' topic. I typically pay the article writer $5, and if they do a substantial job, and over deliver, I tip them well. I tip the good writers very-very-well because I want to keep them excited and happy to work for me in the future (when I need them on a short notice basis). Then what I do is expound on their article, and lengthen it, and add my own flavor and flairs.

See, I'm all about creating value. I don't want my readers (you) reading useless junk that isn't going to help you. I tell it all. I don't cloud or hide the details or secrets like many other product developers do. The reason I do this is to create extreme goodwill in the marketplace so I can dominate my niche. I want happy customers. The customer is number one in my opinion. They pay my bills!

After I have this out of the way, I've created an e-book in a day, and can throw it up on Amazon and wait for the sales to come in. Tomorrow I'll be writing another e-book or doing something else that creates a residual asset.

The most important thing is to always be creating residual assets and do it as fast as humanely possible. Your income is completely depended on your ability to do this one requirement. If you take the day off you've exponentially cheated yourself out of a tremendous amount of income. This is my number one motivation.

Do I take vacations? Do I do fun stuff? Absolutely! I do, but never at the expense of creating a daily residual asset. When I'm on vacation I'll still be working each and every day. I do this because it's a habit you must be in to make it in this freelance industry. You have to be willing to do what your competition isn't willing to do. You have to be willing to get up early and work late into the night, be-cause if you adopt this habit you'll be seeing more and more income each and every month.

I don't know about you, but I don't want to be 'working' for a living; making somebody else rich. I'd rather have my headphones on listening to the music I want to listen to, writing, creating YouTube videos, and blogging. I also like to take longer and more frequent breaks than what a job would ever give me. More than any other reason though is the money is fabulous and I can plan my work around my life; not my life around my work. That's slav-ery in my opinion!

CHAPTER 7

WHAT NEW FREELANCERS TYPICALLY BELIEVE THAT YOU SHOULD NOT

Most new and many experienced freelancers, especially many in foreign countries like India, believe is that you should take a 'workers' mentality to doing freelance. Often times these are the freelancers I hire, because they tend to be more giving than many U.S. and U.K. freelancers.

You see the problem with hiring freelancers in first-world countries as it pertains to my system is that you'll almost always pay more, and you'll have to fight to get the U.S. and U.K. freelancers to deliver high quality content for the same rate that you can get with hiring Indian freelancers, per se.

This may sound absurd, I get know, but you have to understand that U.S. and U.K. workers aren't usually going to work for nothing, whereas Indian freelancers will work for a lot less, as a general rule. I have, to be perfectly honest with you, hired freelancers in India only to have them refuse to work for such a low rate. One guy told me tried to sell me on the idea (he was right actually) that if I paid him a high rater I'd get a better value than hiring another Indian at a lower rate. The reason for this is because the person I hired to do a job for $2 per hour, instead of $5 per hour, didn't have the best grammar or communication skills. I had to go round and round with the $2 guy just to get the quality I was looking for.

Even so, I wasn't pressed for time, and so insisting on a higher quality and many re-writes eventually landed me what I wanted for the lowest rate possible. Had I been in a hurry, I'd of definitely hired the $5 guy, but, and this is huge: don't put yourself in a position to where you have to be in a hurry.

For example: I hired a 27 low wage freelancers last week to work on a project of mine. I only needed nine freelancers to get the job done that I needed. I also knew I would be working on a huge chunk of the work. Here's what I did: I took the work from the first nine that finished acceptable work. This was accomplished by Wednesday. I hired them all on Monday. I then let the others know that I had a deadline to meet and wouldn't be needing their services. This does a couple things: (a) it holds people accountable for quality, even if they lack in skills, (b) it gets what I need done sooner rather than later, and (c) it gives me an opportunity to find the best of the best low wage freelancers that I 'want' to work with on a consistent basis moving into the future. The others, well, they either have to improve on their skillset, or find some other profession.

Like in most businesses: time is money, quality can't be compromised, and you have to find the best value for the lowest rates possible. Mainstream companies do this all the time, because they're competing with some fierce competition, and their shareholder's returns are their primary concern. You have to keep the people funding your enterprise happy, or else they take their money somewhere else. It is business, and for the freelance entrepreneur—it's the same type of scenario.

So what do most freelancers believe when they start working freelance? Well, let's rephrase that to include predominantly freelancers in third and fourth world countries.

I lived in India for several years, and worked for an Indian firm there. The Indian mentality was to put your work before yourself. The work ethics of workers there impressed me. They weren't lazy (the ones I knew anyhow) and they valued and took ownership of their jobs. It was culturally engrained that work, in many respects, was something to be highly valued, because many people in India weren't so fortunate to have a job. When someone got a job, they simply kept it at whatever cost they had to pay. The employers could dump on them, belittle them, criticize them, and treat them really, really, poorly, and they took it without argument, because they valued the job at such a high cost.

The freelancer's I've hired from India have sort of the same worker's mentality. They look at the person they're doing a freelance job for as their employer and they really (in most cases) want to get it right and be accepted and re-hired by the person contracting them to work for them.

I asked a freelancer in India to help me by sharing their ideas about freelance. I asked him to share his insights and opinions and to give advice to new freelancers. Here's what he believes about freelancing:

"Money is the most essential need for a human being to survive, nicely. Without money a person can't have status. Many people do a business to earn money, i.e. freelance jobs, as they believe that doing a job is not sufficient enough to earn a special status symbol. Many believe that having their own company is better than doing a job under a boss. They believe that creating a job is better than finding a job.

"There are many ways of earning money from the Internet. One of the ways is to write articles, blog posts, and do creative writing for websites.

"If you are a beginner and you don't know how or where to start then you should follow some basic points:

I.   "Build your own website. Name the website according to the topics you will write. You can have a domain name from a web host in UK or US. You can make a personal website and start writing blogs and articles on your website.

1.   2. "As the traffic increases on your website, Google and other advertising websites will be attracted towards you and they will provide you money for putting on their advertisements. Please make sure that the content you write is original and creative. This makes traffic on your website more and more.

"This is the unique and simple step of making money sitting at home. This will make you creative and up to date with the general awareness and other social news. Many believe that it is a long process of making money and they want to earn money instantly. Don't you worry, there is also another solution. If you want to make money instantly, then you can apply for freelance jobs. You can add your resume to websites which provides these types of simple blog and article writing jobs. You will be paid per article. The writers are given projects also which have to be completed in a given time. There are many types of freelancer's jobs. Some of which are listed below:

    I.   Article Writing

    II.   Data Analysis

    III.   Online research

    IV.   Copywriting

    V.   Data Entry

    VI.   Editing

"By doing these simple jobs, you will be able to make a little money. Follow some of the simple steps that will make you stand out from the crowd:

    I.   Successful online freelancers will always keep their profiles complete and updated. You should also complete your profile to attract more and more jobs.

    II.   Highlighting your skills is another major factor that will attract jobs. Tell about your strong points and areas. Sell yourself to your employer.

III. Always add your photo; this will make a great impact on the boss's decision to hire you.

IV. Always try to get good feedback from your boss. Eliminate your weaknesses.

Some of the merits of these freelancers' jobs are:

a. You can make money *instantly.*

b. Your knowledge is updated *regularly.*

c. You can save your spare time and get a *handsome salary* from this.

Demerits of these jobs are:

a. Sometimes you have to work on regular basis even on holidays to complete projects.

b. You have to *obey* orders from your boss and have to complete your work on time.

So, choose the suitable freelancer jobs according to your interest and earn some *extra* money without stepping out from your house.

That's the advice given by the freelancer. There's a lot of sound advice, and there's even mention of having your own website. But, part of the expense of freelancing is spending your time doing activities that don't produce much money (if any). This is a trap many people fall into when they decide they want to start as a freelancer. You see, when you're new you want to get those jobs, and are more likely to bid on them so low that you can prove your capabilities to the marketplace to hopefully get your portfolio built up, plus your ranking, and then you think to yourself: "Now I can ask for more money!"

The problem with this mentality is that by the time you've gotten to this place in time, you'll have already went broke and had to deal with crummy people hiring you for next to nothing, and then many of them will rank you low or blackmail you with idea that they'll give you a low ranking if you don't let them have the work you've done for them for free, i.e. cancel out of the job after the fact.

There are a lot of bad experiences that can happen (I'm not saying they will happen). My reason for bringing all this up is to get you to see all this differently. I want you to see who is really profiting, and who is not.

More often than not the freelancer is the one losing out and the person contracting their services is positioning themselves to make a lot of money; paying very little to nothing to do so. You need to be the person on the profit side of all this freelancer stuff, not the side of the unequal equation that is getting taken advantage of.

CHAPTER 8

MOTIVATION

O ne of the biggest problems freelancers face every single day is staying motivated, so that they can continue to produce high quality content. Everybody at some point of their lives, their brain freezes or blocks. Some days it is just hard to stay on top of your game. We all want to be successful, and be able to pay our bills on time. However, with our mind blocked it's too hard to achieve this goals. I am sure there is a lot we can do to stay motivated on our work when it comes to freelancing.

With the cost of living increasing every day, there is definitely the need to look for ways we can motivate ourselves so that we acquire the most income possible freelancing. The first thing we can do is position our mindset differently. This means waking up each morning expectant and grateful for the type of work we do. Too often freelancers will come to dread the work of freelance. This means they'll start to become bored with the same old jobs repeating. This is a valid point, and one that can be addressed by growing your skillset. You may decide to learn a new in-demand skill that will take you away from the same old work you've been doing. Maybe this will be the much needed break to reinvigorate your freelance spirit.

Below are some tips you can use to stay on track of freelancing:

You should have written goals in front of you. Having written goals is a fantastic way to stay motivated. Researchers have found out that writing your goals down completely changes your subconscious mind from negativity or apathy, to a positive influence on your day to today life. When you have clearly written your goals concerning your long-term vision, it will dramatically increase both your quantity and quality of work; leading to greater wealth and abundance.

When you are having trouble, write or do your freelance assignments in bursts. A perfect way to get back to your full swing of things when you have lost motivation, is to set 25 minutes of your time aside to write as fast as possible without worrying about formatting or spelling. The same can be applied to design work, or just about any other freelance type work—for example, editing: You can quit worrying about editing someone's ebook perfectly and instead (at least at first) just make edits on what stands out to you, as quick as possible. You'll be surprised to learn that very often you'll correct most of the assignment that first go round, as you're working subconsciously, and not being overly critical, which can be constraining. If you're writing, just get all your thoughts down and then fix it up later. What you don't know is that this will obviously suppress the analyzing part of a writer's brain that goes back over what he/she has already written to start criticizing it. In a matter of a short while, you will notice your mistakes and you will start to correct them. When one gets to write or type very fast, his/her brain does not get a chance to analyze things; therefore, it allows his/her creativity to have more access.

Ensure you get a routine going. When you wake up in the morning, ensure you get a small routine going which will surely allow your mind and body get into the groove. The routine you choose does not have to be anything very specific per se, it can be anything that you think works for you. You can decide to take a cup of coffee, take a dog for a walk, read a newspaper, just to mention but a few. This will surely help your mind to accept that it is time to write or do some other freelance task. Routines create habits; good habits are what you want.

Last but not least do not have negative friends. A statistics carried out in 2005 showed that an individual is likely to earn an average as the same as his/her 5 closest friends. Therefore, if you need to be motivated to earn a lot of cash, stay away from negative friends who are likely to pull you down to their level. Always associate yourself with people who are positive minded and have a great vision for their life. This cannot be underscored enough.

I mentioned earlier in this book the experience of freelancing with my brother. I told you how he ended up going back into the 'fast-food' workplace. I told you he made more money than I did on a weekly basis (at that time). I have to say, back then at least, it was a hard proposition to pass-up; that is to say, going back into the workforce so I could pay my bills and not have to think too much. And, don't get me wrong, I'm not knocking fast-food jobs, I've done plenty of them in my life time and many of them were fun, financially took care of me, and had their own perks (free food, friends, etc.). Anyway, the experience of working with my brother was negative (although he and I did laugh our butts off a lot after drinking too much coffee, and there was that time when we nearly got kicked out of a local bookstore when we started making sales calls through Skype using their wireless internet connection) and we didn't always see eye-to-eye and for this reason we stayed broke and bitter.

You will likely, if you're not careful, have someone (or more than one person) in your life try and beat you down and naysay everything you do. You have to avoid these people like the plague. Tell them little about what you actually do when you must associate with them, and take nothing they tell you seriously (though let them think you do to pacify them and to get them to shut up). If you look at these type of people chances are they are going anywhere but up in their lives. They may even have a decent paying job, but when you put two and two together with these people you'll quickly realize that they'll only ever have (more likely than not) the same consistent lifestyle that they have, and likely more downs than ups. They are the people who criticize everyone for taking the 'rogue' route to wealth. They themselves I hazard to guess, will never be rich. So why would you want to listen to them anyways? Have a think about this, it's important!

CHAPTER 9

THE ROGUE ROUTE TO WEALTH

That last chapter was more or less a warning for you to stay away from the doubters, and to keep your motivation in check by creating routine habits for yourself. In this chapter I want to present you with a convincing argument for why you can be wealthy by being *playfully mischievous* (one of the definitions of a rogue). I like this definition of a 'rogue' because to me it's the perfect attitude to have is you want to be successful. You can't take yourself too seriously, and you need to have a playfulness about you to endure through the times that are not so fun.

I need you to suspend your disbelief or doubt that you can make a lot of money as a freelancer. I know, perhaps, many of you reading this book have tried before and found it's not all it's cracked up to be. But here's the thing...

In my life, everything great that has ever happened to me has happened as a result of me suspending my disbelief and doubt that it was possible or likely. I mean, when I found the love of my life I found her unexpectedly and simply suspended my doubts about her being the one. We're still together today, happy as ever, and still very much in love.

Another example, I wanted to write a book. It seemed like a difficult and challenging task that I'd never be able to complete. I suspended my disbelief and took a leap of faith and now I'm on book sixteen.

Had I never suspended my disbelief and took a chance I never would have all the great things in my life that I have. I mean...really get this! This is the most important thing I can teach anybody.

A good decision is usually the result of someone suspending their disbelief and doubt and just going for it.

Let's do a thought experiment: Think about something positive you have acquired in your life. Now think back to when it was only a 'possibility' and you had to make a decision one way or the other to go after it or not. Maybe you didn't believe you were worthy, or perhaps you didn't think it was going to happen for you, but you went for it anyway, regardless of your doubts. And, today you have it, don't you.

Now, imagine what would have happened, and how your life would be had you not suspended your disbelief and just gone for it? Had you not taken a leap of faith, or made a 'decision' you wouldn't be where you are today, would you?

Where am I going with all of this? Good question. I have the answer.

When you start freelancing you do it because you want to be able to work independently from your home, and succeed in taking care of yourself, possibly your family. You want it bad, and there's nothing wrong with that. Earning my first dollar independently where I wasn't reliant on a job for my income or my parents, was quite an amazing feeling. When someone realized that I was valuable and was willing to pay for something I knew or could help assist them with *that* was an incredibly empowering day for me. It gave me value, self-esteem, and motivation to continue on in my pursuit of being a freelancer. I felt like I could make money even without a job, and that was liberating...know what I mean?

Then the reality set in, and I realized that a dollar wasn't going to pay my bills. I panicked and people around me noticed my shift in mindset. I even started talking about the possibility and likelihood of needing a job. I couldn't concentrate on doing the freelance jobs I had been commissioned to do, and I was falling into nervousness and despair. I was working much longer than 8 hours per day. I was working from the time I awoke till the time I went to bed at night (often times getting little sleep, feeling exhausted).

I had the worst thoughts happen. I became scared. And then something happened to change all that, something brilliant...

I took my dog for a walk and calmed down. I turned off my thoughts and started seeing the beautiful day in front of me. I felt the breeze, and noticed the birds chirping. I zoned out, and by doing so I found my zone, and my life has never been the same.

I started working in the zone, which simply stated means I work hypnotized. I just do, and don't think, because I know my hypnotic mind can do a much better job of thinking for me. I get more done. I'm always improving and learning more and I enjoy life more. I'm playful with others, not worrying about problems, and instead just an actor in this thing we call life.

A hundred words I write turn into a thousand; a thousand into ten thousand; ten thousand into one hundred thousand. And fast, without thinking about it, it happens. People who know me are amazed by what I'm able to accomplish. They used to be shocked, and many didn't believe me. I have written books in a single day, and designed book covers for them and had them listed up for sale on

Amazon—all of this in only one day! I'll do that with this book in fact.

You have to suspend your disbelief about what you are capable of doing when you get out of the way consciously and allow your unconscious 'hypnotic mind' to take over. You'll get more done in a day than what would take most people a year to do. This is the mindset I want you to have. You have to get out of the way of your thoughts. You have to free your mind, take a walk, clear the air, and do. Action is easy when you take these simple steps.

Until Roger Banister ran the four minute mile, everyone said it was impossible to do. Then after he proved them wrong, by suspending his own disbelief and doubts, he did it, and shortly thereafter others broke the four minute barrier as well. You don't have to believe, you only have to suspend temporarily your disbelief and doubts.

I'm really hitting on the personal development side of things now, aren't I? I'm doing this because this is the Rogue Route to Wealth. You make the impossible look simple. You wisely notice resources in your life that most people wouldn't. You don't think about what's not possible or possible, you simply act in that state of flow and watch others look at you in amazement. This builds extreme motivation and rocket propels you faster and higher than most people. This is the edge you need to be a successful freelancer that is working on achieving wealth faster.

When you suspend your disbelief, others will look at your accomplishments with disbelief. You make the impossible possible and you do it all by being in the flow, playing and smiling your way to the top, and by having an attitude of gratitude.

Find out what puts you in the flow, where you think without thinking consciously, and act without consciously acting, and simple do—then do what it is you do, and watch what happens. You'll be utterly surprised. I know I was. In fact, I still am.

CHAPTER 10

THE SYSTEM'S BLUEPRINT

Now we get into a plan of attack. Again, I want you thinking for yourself. This is the way I was able to become a rich freelancer, and I believe it is the only way to go, if you ask me. That being said, you need something to follow to keep you from getting distracted as you build your residual freelance empire. Also, keep in mind that my strategy can be modified, I believe, and still have you coming up on top and creating a great deal of passive residual wealth for yourself. I'm also going to share with you some ideas I've had, but have fallen short on, which I sort of regret not taking more seriously. Perhaps you'll want to do a better job in these areas than I did. You may find yourself becoming wealthier sooner.

So first things first: I want to give you the system blueprint that I personally used. If you follow it, and work it as I have, I have no doubt that you won't make it as a freelancer, and in the process create wealth for yourself. This being said, I'm not making any claims in this book, as I don't know you, your personal situation, nor can I predict the future or viability of this system in the future.

The first thing I did was set up a lot of freelance accounts. I did originally what most people did, but only because I didn't know any better. This was simply to go onto all the major freelance sites and set up accounts, build a profile, on some of the freelance sites you can take 'skills tests' to help you achieve better profile ranking, as well some of the freelance sites provide you with more opportunities to bid on jobs with more skills tests completed. The advice I would give you is to take your time with this part of the strategy. Make sure all your profiles have a very nice photo of yourself. I would go so far as to hire a professional photographer to take the photos for you, so you can instantly stand out from the crowd, and get noticed.

The next thing I did was to set up a personal blog. I used a self-hosted WordPress blog, and created it for the purpose of sharing information freely with others that had a high value element to it. I came from a sales and marketing background, so for me I took my skills and knowledge and applied it in this direction. You can use something business related that has value, or something that is more specialized and more your passion. I highly recommend that your blog consist of two things: (a) make sure it is something you are passionate about, and (b) make sure it is a topic that other people are interested. You cannot go wrong usually with 'money making strategies', 'health and wellness secrets', and broad areas that people generally tend to be interested in.

Make sure your 'about page' on your blog matches your profile on your freelance sites. This creates brand recognition and when people who are thinking about hiring you for a job visit your website they will usually check this page out. Next, make sure you have your portfolio of 'best' work listed on your blog. This is so prospective buyers of your freelance service will get a good sense of what your capabilities are. The more excited you can make them with what you've previously done, the more comfortable and likely they will hire you to work on their projects. This blog is the corporate headquarters of your blogging empire. It will constantly be updated as you complete more and more jobs for other buyers/requesters of your service. Also, this blog, because it is yours will be in the buyer's eyes the real you, irrespective of what comments other buyers have left on your freelance profiles.

Once you have this setup I recommend keeping your blog posts regular. You should get in the habit of blogging every day. This routine habit will help your blog to rank faster, and keep prospective and former buyers of your services engaged and reminded of your quality and professionalism.

People want to know you, and for this reason I recommend blogging from the first person perspective. Write your feelings, ideas, insights, and keep everything 100%

positive. People want to hire positive and successful people to work for them, because they believe doing so will mean that your success will rub off onto their business. This creates tremendous value for them, and brands you as someone that 'everybody' can't wait to hire. You can also command a higher price for your services; not that this is where the real wealth comes into play at.

After you've done all this it is time to do what most freelancers don't. It is time to create massive action in the direction of setting up residual assets. You'll want to setup a profile and have a presences on every social media site out there. You definitely want a Facebook fan page, YouTube channel, Twitter account, etc. These should all be connected back to your blog. A way of looking at this setup is to think of a bicycle wheel. There is a center and from that center are many, many, spokes that lead off into all sorts of different directions. Each of these various directions are represent a residual asset. All of them, however, lead back to the center of the wheel. Your blog is the center, and your YouTube channel, Facebook page, etc. are the residual assets, which are actually opportunities for you to earn a passive residual income.

This takes time, but not that much time to setup. You have to take massive action and get it done as soon as humanely possible. In time you'll also want to set up multiples of each of these accounts. You'll want multiple YouTube channels, Multiple Facebook pages, Multiple

Twitter accounts, etc. The reason being is you'll be connecting with many marketplaces, and each of these represents a unique demographic with different psychographic qualities. You don't sell meat to vegetarians...get the point!

You want to have everything connected back to your blog, which is a general abstraction of who you are and what values you represent. You want to be very general about what you tell about yourself, and what you promote, because you don't want to offend or be off-putting to anyone in particular who might learn about you from one of these various residual assets. For example, if you are a huge proponent of vegetarian idealism, and talk in terms of hate messages towards meat eaters, wishing them all a bumpy road to hell, then you'll be disconnected from meat eaters, who might become offended by your rhetoric, and therefore you lose them as potential customers. That could, and likely would, mean a loss of a great deal of revenue.

The name of this game is money. It's not about proselytizing about your beliefs and values. People, though they may care, they care more about what their own interests, beliefs, and values are: So leave yours at the door with this strategy.

Next, you want to get organized. This means having in one central document all your user names and passwords for all of your online accounts. Keep adding to this list as you go. Whenever you're asked to change your password, update it on your list with the corresponding username and account. Have your profile and resume also readily available. This will make life much easier and wealth faster, because you'll only need to cut-and-paste your profile and resume into the next freelance account, or next social media profile. Everything needs to be nice and uniform. When someone Googles you they need to see only one picture of you on Google images, and on all the different websites and accounts you have. This will help make you unforgettable in the eyes of your publics. Building your brand is much quicker when you uniformly brand yourself the same everywhere.

You can do a simple Google search for the online freelance marketplaces; however, to get you started check out:

Fiverr.com
oDesk.com
Freelancer.com
WarriorForum.com
eLance.com
PeoplePerHour.com
iWriter.com

These sites are a good start, but don't end here. The more freelance sights you have setup, the more chances you have of getting hired. Also, keep in mind that you want to maintain your ratings on these sights so AL-WAYS do a fantastic job for your clients. You'll also, by having multiple accounts setup learn where the cheapest help is and the most expensive help. This will come in handy as you set up your own products for selling, to earn a residual income off from.

Once you've gotten organized it is time to take massive action daily. This means structuring your day to get the most amount of work done possible. 80% of your work day should be in setting up residual assets, only 20% should be doing actual freelance jobs for people. For this reason, only take jobs that allow you to be able to do this. Those long assignments that have short time frames I would personally stay away from. The quick and easy jobs (e.g., 500 word article writing) I would embrace. It's not about the money you make freelancing, it's about the quantity of residual assets you have set up. The sooner you set up these assets the sooner the real money will start rolling in.

Also, a huge word of caution: Many of you reading this may have dabbled in network marketing, or MLMs. This is cool, but don't put yourself in a position where you have your down line calling you all the time for FREE SUPPORT. Instead get my book: *The Essential Guide for Network Marketing*, and apply the principles and advice in it. You can pick it up on Amazon.com here: http://amzn.com/0989946479. If you spend too much time on the phone giving free advice away you'll be personally losing out on tons of money, because it's less time you are setting up those residual assets.

For setting up residual assets I did clickbank.com offers, commissionjunction.com offers, ioffer.com, ebay.com, amazon.com, smashwords.com, ejunkie.com, sellfy.com, my own blog, google pay per click, facebook.com pay per click, social media sites, and I'm a lover of youtube.com. I intertwine these accounts. I will do a four minute youtube.com video in the morning with an introduction to a clickbank.com affiliate offer, or one of my own launch offers, and in the comments section below, I'll paste in the affiliate link. Whenever someone views the video (the video is left on there forever) they will click the affiliate link and buy, and I get a commission. Of course, as you might imagine, the more of these you have the more money you'll be making in any given month. The income, your income, that is, should only continue escalating upwards. You should make more money next month than you do this month, because, again, you're taking 'massive' action.

The next habit I orchestrated into my daily routine was capitalizing on everything. If I had a friend call me, I video skyped it and put what was appropriate on youtube.com, my blog, and other video hosting sites, and added my affiliate links appropriately. This way I had my fun conversation, and took a break from working, and still worked indirectly. Everything I do has a clear purpose of making me more money. There's no reason not to adopt this habit, because you can make money having fun, and in my opinion this is the best way to make money.

If you take a trip out to the lake for a day trip or over-night camping excursion, take your video camera and record the venture and talk about the products you're using, which incidentally are ones you have affiliate deals to market. Take people into your life, and make money living, and you'll make a lot of money.

See, people have it in their minds (most people I've met) that taking a vacation is to get away from work, but when your work is fun, and you're always on vacation, then you start to see how much fun life is and how profitable.

If you're doing a freelance job for a client online, use a screencast software to record your working on the project, and let your personality and comments create interest. After you're finished with the project and have gotten paid on it, put the video on youtube.com and again add in an affiliate offer or a link back to your freelance profile. Get in the habit of capitalizing off of everything. There is so much money to be had if you just master this simple habit.

My Regrets

I told you I was guilty of something, and that I wish I had improved on this much earlier in my freelance embarkation. I wish to goodness sake I had started a 'list'. A list simply refers to a double-opt-in auto-responder list. You can use a paid service like Aweber.com, GetResponse.com, ConstantContact.com, etc. What you want to do is collect the names and emails of everybody that makes a purchase from you, visits your blog, etc.

I didn't do this and regret it every single day. The wealth that comes from having a long list of emails is incredible. Whenever I launch a new product launch, write a new book, discover a new offer that has incredible value, I sent a broadcast email out to all the people on my list. In other words, I write one compelling email, and hit a button and it magically ends up in the email inboxes of all the people on my list. What this does is create massive sales opportunities for you. Having a long list is like owning your own ATM stocked with a never ending supply of free money.

I currently have a MASSIVE list, but I didn't start building from the get-go, or it would be much longer than it is now. There's money in the list. Remember this!

I recommend you get started from day one building a list. You must make sure you follow the laws when it comes to sending out solicitation emails or else you'll have the FCC and FTC breathing down your back. You can even get sued. So do your due-diligence first.

A freelancer is a self-employed person that sometimes is represented by an agency or company. The word "free" means you are free to work for this job in your available time. Years ago, I was sceptic about online jobs and I have done various part- time jobs, but when I first signed on to the freelancer lifestyle and understood the way it works I got totally impressed and excited. If you are a new freelancer from the United States of America, the advice I give in this book will be very helpful for you.

Since I live in the United States of America, the cost of living is significantly higher than in countries like India, Pakistan, and Indonesia etc. So my bids on freelance websites were always more expensive than people from these countries, and hence I rarely got a job during the first days as a new freelancer. But later, I found out some fields where I made a lot of money and decided to give up my thoughts of going back into the workforce and become a full time freelancer. As a freelancer you may choose the clients you want to work with. You will gain new skills that you won't learn as a traditional employee. Working from your home saves your hours in travel time, the stress of paying outlays of cash to fuel, car maintenance etc. Freelancers are known for their work-life harmony. You may spend a lot of time with your family and friends and more free time to do the things you love. But, remember the principle that you should always be making money, even when you're spending time with friends and family. There's no reason not to. Working from your home can provide some tax benefits such as from home office space, business costs and equipment. A lot of stuff you'd buy anyway for personal use, you can write off as a business owner.

First off, I would recommend you to focus on writing. There are plenty of writing jobs on freelancer, especially if native US language is a requirement for writing articles. But you can also try other fields such as graphic design, transcription work, and being a virtual assistant. A virtual assistant is a way you can finish your job from the help of some other people that are professional. Virtual assistants complete a variety of tasks—for example, article marketing, phone reception, data entry, email responding. If you consider that you are able to do that, then you should begin bidding on the project of the virtual assistant. I have done this type of job on freelance websites like oDesk.com and I can say that I got really satisfied and learned a lot about things I had no clue about. You will get paid depending on the nature and size of the work you did. The average can be $200 per project. Not a bad payday, but definitely not as good as the money you'll be earning from your residual assets soon.

After focusing on what you think you can do best, always be careful to look at the employer's profile and rating or feedback if there is any. If the profile looks doubtful, there's no guarantee of accuracy or that you'll even get paid in some instances.

Once you've checked the profile of the employer and you decide to bid on that project, make an effort to write a nice and professional proposal. Some employers don't even bother to read the proposal, but it won't take you a lot of time to write some few lines.

If you are lucky and get a project award, then before accepting it be careful to read again the project details, because sometimes it is better to pass up a project than to be unsecure about it.

Another tip that I would recommend is to stay active and not become anti-social with your offline contacts. Joining a professional group can also be beneficial so long as it doesn't detract from you making money. Marketing yourself can be a bit tough for a new freelancer, but it is an extremely crucial component of getting new jobs.

Overall, I can say that if you are a new United States freelancer you can use many strategies to generate better income, and why not do so, and make a full time living as a freelancer. Furthermore, there are various and simple payment options such as: PayPal, Check, Credit Card, Money Order, and Wire Transfer. More often than not you don't have to wait on your money. This is a refreshing experience for those of you who are accustomed to getting paid every two weeks by your employer. It's my money; I want it NOW!

The last part of this system's blueprint is to hire outsourcers to do a lot of the product development work you don't want to do, or have limited skills in being able to accomplish. If you want to write a book, and quickly, you can hire freelance writers to write articles that you can turn into chapters, by expounding on them a little. You can hire a graphic designer for cheap to make a book cover for your book. You have a lot of leverage hiring freelancers, and once your book is finished and listed up on Amazon, you will make money off of it like any other residual asset. Just, again, don't forget about the principle of massive action. You need to do things quick and get the money rolling in, so you can go on to creating another new residual asset. The more of these assets you have working for you, the less work you have to do.

Everything I'm telling you in this book is doable. You can do this! You have what it takes! You have to make it happen though.

PLEASE READ

The freelance system I've shared with you in this book worked for me. I hope it works for you as well. There's no better feeling in the world in my opinion than making money doing nothing. Residual assets allow you to do that. They are only (for the most part) an investment of your time and the leveraged time of the freelancers you hire to do much of the work aspects you don't want to do or don't feel comfortable doing.

The idea is to take massive action and setup these residual assets as you're learning new skills working as a freelancer so that you can 'forget-it' and let the money roll on in on autopilot. As I've sat here today, at my computer writing this book, I just noticed ten minutes ago an alert popup letting me know I had just earned another affiliate commission for a product I don't even own, but marketed years ago on another person's website. The forty-five dollars may not seem like a lot, but I have made many multiple $45 dollar payments from this one affiliate link that I set up so very long ago. It's made me thousands of dollars over time, and it's only one residual asset out of many, many, thousands I've set up over the years. You can do the same.

The benefits for me personally is that I get to travel and live in foreign countries of my choice for as long as I desire. I don't have to have a job to support my lifestyle. I only have to keep building my residual empire, and the money keeps growing month after month.

When I was younger I worked and invested in stocks and real estate, and I can tell you from this vantage point that I will make more money with less upfront investment doing what I do now, than I could ever hope to make from those more traditional investments. I know this from experience. I'm much more diversified on my residual asset portfolio and have never, since adopting this approach I've shared with you, ever wanted for anything. Life is terrific!

My advantage has always been other people's lack of action and inability to take stock of their resources. I get a lot of criticism, but I laugh my way to the bank, while those who criticize stress out driving in rush hour traffic to get to work in time, before their boss hands them a pink slip, and smiles at them.

I'll tell you how all of this came about for me. I mean came about before I quit my sales job. Listen, a long time ago I faced a certain problem. It was a painful problem. I wanted to live abroad in a foreign country and survive and not have to worry about earning money. I didn't have rich parents or much money. I simply wanted to live where I wanted to live, but without foregoing my U.S. citizenship. I looked into ways to solve the problem. I found few options that would work, and the ones I did, meant an unenjoyable experience. This problem wouldn't leave me. But, life continued. The thought kept resurfacing time and time again throughout periods of my life. I am a natural problem solver, but couldn't seem to manage to solve this problem.

I eventually, solved it though. It was through freelance working, and while doing so building up a ton of residual assets. I needed money coming in, even if I couldn't work. I mean, after all, accidents happen, people get sick, life happens, and so what I wanted was a means to financially take care of myself should I run into anything that would hinder my ability to work and make money. The liberation that this system I have shared with you in this book has brought to my life is priceless.

I hope it becomes priceless for you as well. You absolutely deserve the best that life has to offer, and it's definitely possible to have the best. The questions you need to ask yourself now is, Will I be one of the rare breeds who takes massive action and make it happen for myself? Will suspend my disbelief and doubts and take the leap of faith into the world of possibilities, which lead to success? Will

I be relentless in setting up residual asset investments for myself that will pay me long into the future?

Have a think on that!

Learn Well! Live Well!

Bryan Westra

www.indirectknowledge.com

bryan@indirectknowledge.com

Bibliography

P. T. Barnum. The Art of Money Getting; Or, Golden Rules for Making Money (Kindle Locations 372-374).

P. T. Barnum. The Art of Money Getting; Or, Golden Rules for Making Money (Kindle Locations 314-315).

Index

ABOUT THE AUTHOR

BRYAN WESTRA is a freelancer and the founder of Indirect Knowledge Limited. For more information about him please visit: www.indirectknowledge.com.